JAPAN

Explore the Countries

Julie Murray

Big Buddy BOOKS
Explore the Countries

VISIT US AT
www.abdopublishing.com

Published by ABDO Publishing Company, PO Box 398166, Minneapolis, MN 55439.

Printed in the United States of America, North Mankato, Minnesota.
032013
092013

 PRINTED ON RECYCLED PAPER

Coordinating Series Editor: Rochelle Baltzer
Editor: Sarah Tieck
Contributing Editors: Megan M. Gunderson, Marcia Zappa
Graphic Design: Adam Craven
Cover Photograph: *Shutterstock*: Filip Fuxa.
Interior Photographs/Illustrations: *Alamy*: Photos 12 (p. 27); *AP Photo*: AP Photo (p. 33), Imaginechina via AP Images (p. 17), Shizuo Kambayashi (p. 27), Kyodo News (p. 29), Luong Thai Linh, Pool (p. 19), The Yomiuri Shimbun via AP Images (p. 19); *Getty Images*: Tomohiro Ohsumi/Bloomberg via Getty Images (p. 25); *Glow Images*: Rex Butcher (p. 35), Chad Ehlers (p. 37), © Eye Ubiquitous (p. 34), The Print Collector (p. 31), SuperStock (pp. 13, 25), Werner Forman Archive/C.D. Wertheim Collection Werner Forman Archive Werner Forman (p. 16); *iStockphoto*: ©iStockphoto.com/prasit_chansareekorn (p. 5); *Shutterstock*: Neale Cousland (p. 9), Filip Fuxa (p. 23), Globe Turner (pp. 19, 38), jonson (p. 34), Ko. Yo (p. 11), koi88 (p. 35), murata-photo com (p. 21), N.F. Photography (p. 15), redswept (p. 23), Lisa S. (p. 38), Tupungato (p. 11), YuryZap (p. 35).

Country population and area figures taken from the CIA World Factbook.

Library of Congress Control Number: 2013932174

Cataloging-in-Publication Data

Murray, Julie.
Japan / Julie Murray.
　p. cm. -- (Explore the countries)
ISBN 978-1-61783-815-6 (lib. bdg.)
1. Japan--Juvenile literature.   I. Title.
952--dc23

2013932174

Contents

AROUND THE WORLD

Our world has many countries. Each country has different land. It has its own rich history. And, the people have their own languages and ways of life.

Japan is a country in Asia. What do you know about Japan? Let's learn more about this place and its story!

Did You Know?

Japanese is the official language of Japan. The words are drawn with symbols or characters that represent sounds. In Japanese, the word *Japan* is written 日本.

Mount Fuji is a famous volcano in Japan. At 12,388 feet (3,776 m), it is the country's highest peak.

PASSPORT TO JAPAN

Japan is located in the Pacific Ocean. It is off the east coast of Asia. Russia, China, and North and South Korea are nearby.

Japan is made up of many islands. The four major islands are Hokkaido, Honshu, Shikoku, and Kyushu.

Japan has a total area of 145,914 square miles (377,915 sq km). More than 127 million people live there!

SAY IT

Hokkaido
haw-KEYE-doh

Shikoku
shee-KOH-koo

Honshu
HAHN-shoo

Kyushu
KYOO-shoo

WHERE IN THE WORLD?

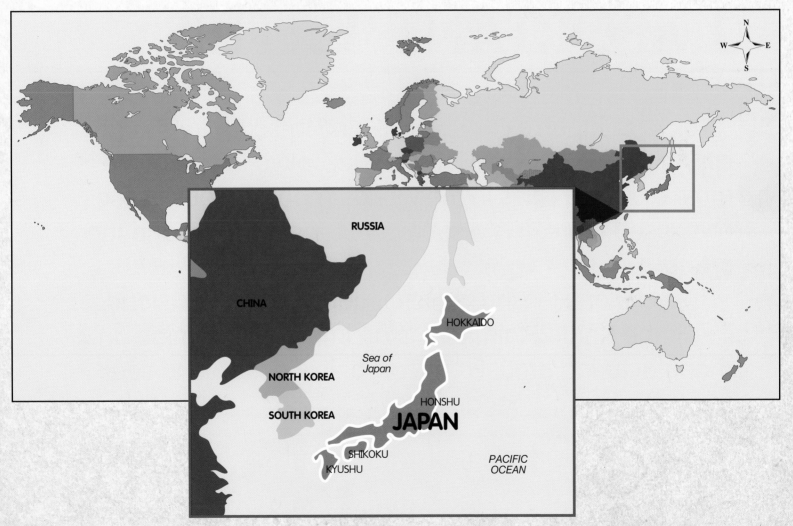

IMPORTANT CITIES

Tokyo is Japan's **capital**. It is also the country's largest city, with about 8.9 million people. Tokyo is one of the most crowded cities in the world. Important businesses are based there. It is also known for education and the arts.

Tokyo is on Honshu, which is Japan's largest island. It is in the Kanto Plain. This is an important farming and manufacturing area. From Tokyo, it is possible to see Mount Fuji on a clear day.

Did You Know?

Tokyo began in 1457. Japanese traditions are still very much a part of this modern city.

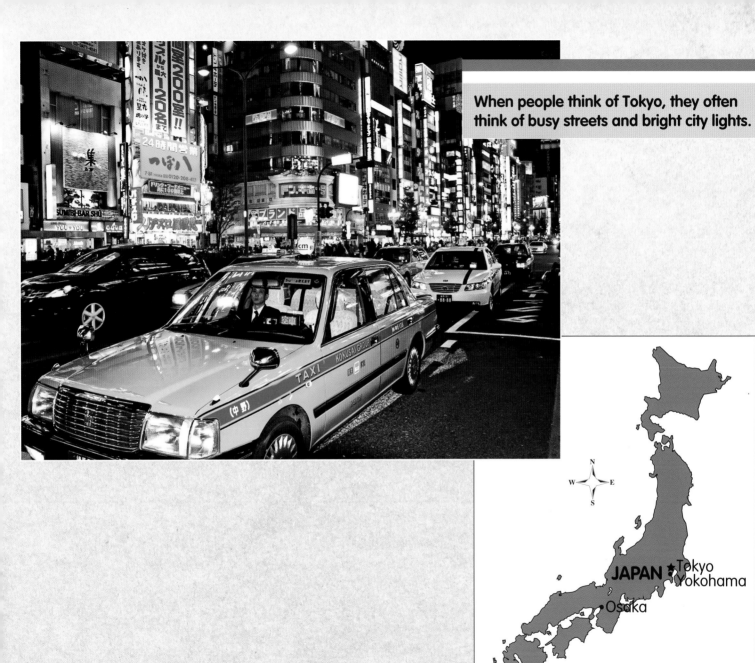

When people think of Tokyo, they often think of busy streets and bright city lights.

JAPAN

★Tokyo
Yokohama
Osaka

Yokohama is Japan's second-largest city. It is home to about 3.7 million people. Many goods pass through the city's ports and railroad lines. Ships, cars, and other products are made there.

Osaka is Japan's third-largest city, with about 2.7 million people. Both Yokohama and Osaka are located on Honshu. Osaka is on Osaka Bay and the Yodo River. It is known for making products such as clothes.

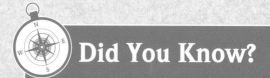

Did You Know?

Many people in Osaka live in tall apartment buildings. Some shopping areas are underground because there is limited land for building.

Yokohama has many gardens, parks, and universities. But, it is also very crowded.

Osaka has canals and rivers. It is known for having good seafood.

Japan in History

The first people to settle in Japan were hunters and gatherers. Thousands of years later, many families farmed rice. Around 600, Japan began to use ideas from China. These included **Buddhism**, writing, and a central government.

Throughout history, powerful family groups fought to rule Japan. Being an island helped keep Japan safe from other countries. But, fighting inside kept it from growing.

Around 1100, noble warriors called samurai became powerful. In 1192, warlords called shoguns began ruling Japan. But, samurai continued to fight for power.

Did You Know?

Around 800, the arts grew in Japan. The country's writers began creating books. Artists wrote poetry and painted.

Samurai were skilled with swords. Early samurai protected the wealthy and were part of the country's military.

Around 1600, shoguns limited trade with other countries. This lasted until the 1850s.

Shoguns stopped ruling Japan around 1867, when Emperor Meiji took power. Under Emperor Meiji, Japan began to change. A new school system and a new central government were created. By the 1900s, Japan had grown powerful and modern with skilled workers.

Japan suffered much in **World War II**. But, the people worked hard to rebuild. Today, the country is known for its strong businesses.

Himeji Castle is a famous historic castle. It was built in the 1300s in traditional Japanese style.

Timeline

1185

The Minamoto clan set up a military government. The first shogun began ruling Japan in 1192.

794

Heian-kyo became the capital. Later it became known as Kyoto.

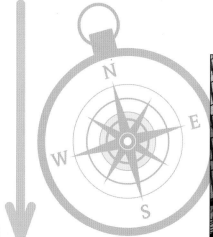

1853

Matthew Perry of the United States went to Japan with warships. He ordered Japan to trade goods with the United States. Soon, Japan agreed.

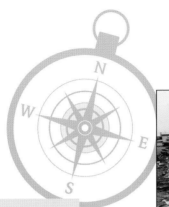

1868

Tokyo became Japan's **capital**.

2011

A large **earthquake** struck near Honshu's coast. It caused a **tsunami**. Thousands of people died in this disaster.

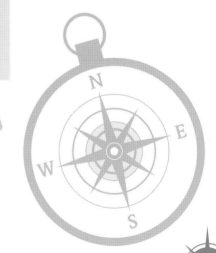

1945

The United States dropped **atomic bombs** on the cities of Hiroshima and Nagasaki. This killed more than 100,000 people. It led to the end of **World War II**.

AN IMPORTANT SYMBOL

Japan's flag was adopted in 1854. It has a red sun on a white background. This was chosen because the country's people call Japan *Nippon*. This means "source of sun."

In Japan, the prime minister leads the government. Laws are made by a group called the Diet. The country still has an emperor. But, he has little power today.

Did You Know?

Japan has political areas called prefectures. These are like small states.

Japan's flag is flown during important events.

Prime Minister Abe Shinzo took office in 2012.

Emperor Akihito and Empress Michiko are part of Japan's imperial, or royal, family. Akihito became emperor in 1989. He is the 125th in this family line.

ACROSS THE LAND

Japan has mountains, hills, forests, waterfalls, and coasts. It is in a part of the world known for having **volcanoes** and **earthquakes**. Japan has about 60 active volcanoes. And, there may be 1,500 small earthquakes each year.

Japan has many small rivers and lakes. The Sea of Japan is on Japan's western side. The Pacific Ocean is to the east.

Did You Know?

In August, the average temperature in southern and central Japan is 86°F (30°C). In January, it is 46°F (8°C). Northern Japan and areas high in the mountains are usually much cooler.

The Japanese Alps on Honshu are Japan's highest mountains.

Many types of animals make their homes in Japan. These include Japanese black bears, wild boars, and a type of monkey called the Japanese macaque. Swans and cranes live there, too. There are also turtles, snakes, and hundreds of types of fish.

Japan is known for its forests. Plants found there include spruce trees, fir trees, and bamboos.

Many macaques live near hot springs in Nagano on Honshu.

Bamboo can grow as tall as a tree.
But, it is actually a type of grass.

EARNING A LIVING

Japan is known for manufacturing and trade. Computers and cars are some of the products made there. Also, many people work in service jobs. These include working for banks or the government.

Japan has some natural **resources**. It is a world leader in fishing. Oysters and seaweed also come from its waters. Farmers in Japan produce rice, potatoes, and eggs.

Rice farmers work in rice paddies.

Cars are built in Japan's factories.

LIFE IN JAPAN

Japan's people are known for valuing the past. They have great respect for older people.

People in Japan are also known for eating light foods. Seafood and rice are very common.

Many Japanese people take part in **Shinto** or **Buddhist** events and **rituals**. These have been part of life in Japan for centuries. People visit shrines or temples to pray. During festivals, people attend parades and carry fans. They may wear long robes called kimonos.

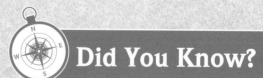

Did You Know?

In Japan, children may attend school on weekends. The school year begins in April and goes almost year-round.

Kites have been popular in Japan for hundreds of years.

Anime and manga are popular art forms in Japan.

Sumo wrestling is Japan's national sport. Attending matches is a popular activity there. Most matches last less than one minute.

Sumo wrestlers fight in a ring called a *dohyo*. In the ring, wrestlers must not touch the ground with anything but the bottoms of their feet. Also, they must not leave the ring. The first person to fall or leave the ring loses.

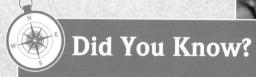

Did You Know?

Sumo wrestling is an ancient sport in Japan. It includes many Shinto rituals.

Sumo wrestlers are famous for their size. Gaining weight is part of their training. They often eat a hearty meat and vegetable soup called *chanko-nabe*.

FAMOUS FACES

Japan's history has many strong leaders. Emperor Meiji was born in Kyoto on November 3, 1852. His given name was Mutsuhito.

For hundreds of years, military leaders called shoguns ruled Japan. In 1867, Meiji became emperor. He worked with nobles and samurai to change Japan's government.

Under Emperor Meiji, Japan set up a modern army and navy. Japan also made schools and businesses more modern. Soon, the country was known worldwide for its skill and strength. In 1912, Meiji died.

Meiji served as Japan's emperor until his death.

Emperor Hirohito was born in Tokyo on April 29, 1901. He was the son of Emperor Taisho. So, he grew up learning about politics and ruling a country.

Hirohito became emperor in 1926. He was Japan's leader during **World War II**. When Japan **surrendered**, the US Army took control of the country. Later, Japan was governed by elected officials. Hirohito had lost power, but he remained emperor until his death in 1989.

Hirohito traveled outside Japan before and during his rule. He was the first member of his family to do this!

Tour Book

Have you ever been to Japan? If you visit the country, here are some places to go and things to do!

 ## Explore

Check out Kyoto's Gion festival in July. It has been held for more than 1,000 years! It includes parades, foods, and traditional clothing.

Eat

Try some sushi! Nigiri-zushi is an oval of rice topped with raw seafood such as octopus or eel. Maki-zushi has rice, vegetables, and seafood rolled in seaweed.

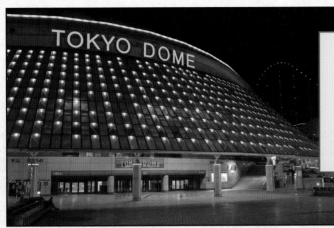

Cheer

Take in a baseball game at the Tokyo Dome. The Yomiuri Giants often play there. The dome also hosts many large concerts.

Remember

Visit Peace Memorial Park in Hiroshima. Check out the museum and learn about the atomic bomb that destroyed the city. There are also activities to promote peace.

Discover

Go to a Kabuki play! This is a type of Japanese play known for colorful costumes and makeup. Some audience members even wear kimonos!

A Great Country

The story of Japan is important to our world. The people and places that make up this country offer something special. They help make the world a more beautiful, interesting place.

Japan is known for its colorful festivals. The Aoi festival is held every May. People come from all over the world to see this event in Kyoto.

Japan Up Close

Official Name: Nippon or Nihon (Japan)

Flag:

Population (rank): 127,368,088
(July 2012 est.)
(10th most-populated country)

Total Area (rank): 145,914 square miles
(62nd largest country)

Capital: Tokyo

Official Language: Japanese

Currency: Yen

Form of Government: Parliamentary
democracy with ceremonial emperor

National Anthem: "Kimigayo"
(The Reign of Our Emperor)

Important Words

atomic bomb (uh-TAH-mihk BAHM) a bomb that uses the energy of atoms. Atoms are tiny particles that make up matter.

Buddhism (BOO-dih-zuhm) a religion based on the teachings of Buddha.

capital a city where government leaders meet.

earthquake (UHRTH-kwayk) a shaking of a part of the earth.

resource a supply of something useful or valued.

ritual (RIH-chuh-wuhl) a formal act or set of acts that is repeated.

Shinto a Japanese religion in which people worship ancestors and nature gods.

surrender to give up.

tsunami (soo-NAH-mee) a group of powerful ocean waves that can destroy areas.

volcano a deep opening in Earth's surface from which hot liquid rock or steam comes out.

World War II a war fought in Europe, Asia, and Africa from 1939 to 1945.

Web Sites

To learn more about Japan, visit ABDO Publishing Company online. Web sites about Japan are featured on our Book Links page. These links are routinely monitored and updated provide the most current information available.

www.abdopublishing.com

Index